Skira Guides

Anna Maria Spiazzi

Giotto
The Scrovegni Chapel in Padua

Texts by
Giuseppe Basile and Serenella Borsella

Cover
Left
Giotto, *The Baptism of Christ*, detail
Center
Giotto, *The Last Judgment*, detail
Right
Giotto, *The Ascension*, detail

Art director
Marcello Francone

Editing
Monica Maroni

Layout
Lorena Biffi
Monica Temporiti

Translations
Language Consulting Congressi, Milano

Photographic credits
Istituto Centrale per il Restauro, Roma

The photographs were taken
by Angelo Rubino on behalf
of the Istituto Centrale per il Restauro

First published in Italy in 2004
by Skira Editore S.p.A.
Palazzo Casati Stampa
via Torino 61
20123 Milano
Italy
www.skira.net

© 2004 by Istituto Centrale
per il Restauro, Roma
© 2004 by Skira editore, Milano

Printed and bound in Italy. First edition

ISBN 88-8491-848-0

Distributed in North America and Latin
America by Rizzoli International
Publications, Inc. through St. Martin's
Press, 175 Fifth Avenue, New York,
NY 10010.
Distributed elsewhere in the world by
Thames and Hudson Ltd., 181a High
Holborn, London WC1V 7QX,
United Kingdom.

Contents

Giotto: Biographical Overview

Anna Maria Spiazzi

Giotto, the son of Bondone, was born at Vespignano in the Mugello Valley in 1267, or in 1276 according to some accounts. Vasari relates that Cimabue, on his way from Florence to Vespignano, encountered the ten-year-old Giotto drawing a sheep from nature on a stone, and was so impressed by his skill that he asked the boy to become his pupil. Vasari's story alludes to Giotto's early training, which he undoubtedly received from Cimabue in Florence. During the years of his education in Florence, moreover, the young Giotto must have been exposed to new creative stimuli from the master mosaicists active in the baptistery, as well as coming into contact with the new ideas that found expression in the works of Nicola and Giovanni Pisano in Pisa and Siena.

Giotto's debut in Rome has been identified by Pietro Toesca (1904) in the *Apostles* set in tondi in Santa Maria Maggiore (*c.* 1285-86), which show all the marks of a young and diligent artist working in a style somewhere between those of Cimabue and Arnolfo di Cambio. Pope Nicholas III and his successor Nicholas IV were responsible for a far-reaching renewal of the city of Rome, and Arnolfo, with the ciborium in the basilica of San Paolo (1285), introduced a new approach to the realization of architectural-sculptural works.

After the period in Rome, the young Giotto was active in the upper church of San Francesco in Assisi.

The basilica, on which work had started in 1228, was completed and consecrated in 1253 by Pope Innocent IV. The decoration of the upper church, which had been commenced in the right transept by the "Master from beyond the Mountains" in a markedly Gothic style, was continued in the apse, left transept and vaults by Cimabue, at the beginning of the 1280s or at the end of the same decade (Bel-

Giotto, *Cross*,
Padua, Musei
Civici, Museo d'Arte

9

losi 1985). The decoration of the nave got under way in 1288, at the start of Nicholas IV's pontificate, and was carried out by a team of painters headed by the Roman Jacopo Torriti (Tomei 1990), who realized the first two bays, the vault and the upper part of the third bay on the right. The work was continued by a profoundly innovative painter, of Roman and Florentine formation, with the help of several assistants. The majority of art historians recognize the hand of Giotto in the *Legend of Isaac*, two scenes painted around 1290 in which space is handled in an unprecedented manner and the figures have a new solidity. Others have seen them as the work of Cavallini. Giotto's activity in Assisi, recorded by Riccobaldo Ferrarese (1312), is also explicitly mentioned by Ghiberti (*c.* 1450): Giotto "painted almost all the lower part in the church of the Order of Friars Minor at Assisi." The date, over which there has been much debate, must have been *ante* 1297 as there are precise citations of the paintings in Assisi in the cycle of frescoes in the Sala dei Notai of the Palazzo dei Priori at Perugia (Bellosi 1982). In addition, Giotto was engaged in the decoration of the loggia of the Lateran in Rome in that year.

The innovations introduced in the *Legend of Saint Francis* are many, commencing with the iconography. This was almost certainly decided on by the Franciscan pope Nicholas IV, who wanted to celebrate St. Francis as the mainstay of the Church and, as a consequence, underline the central role of the Franciscan Order in ecclesiastical life. The approach to the representation of space is also totally new since the scenes, in groups of three, are inserted in a loggia divided up by elegant spiral columns supporting the ceiling. The definition of architectural space in the individual scenes was made the subject of continual research because the figures in each episode had to be able to move within these settings in a manner that was as close to reality as possible. The figures are characterized by a high degree of expressiveness. The episodes are presented as contemporary events and reproduce the style of clothing, the precious fabrics that furnished the papal court, the church vestments and ornaments and the urban views and landscapes of the end of the 13th century.

Such famous scenes as the *Preaching to the Birds*, *Miracle of the Spring*, *Crib at Greccio* and *Appearance of Saint Francis at the Chapter in Arles* are among the finest examples of early Italian painting. And the role played by Giotto in founding the new language of painting was immortalized by Dante: "Cimabue thought to hold the field in painting, and now Giotto hath the cry, so that the other's fame is growing dim" (*Purgatory*, canto XI, 94-6).

Around seven years passed between Giotto's activity in Assisi and the start of the work in Padua, in which the artist attained full maturity in his handling of form, light and color. The information available to us is scanty: we know that he was present at Pope Boniface VIII's court in Rome, and then in Florence, in 1301. However, there are a number of works in which the critics have identified the course of development of Giotto's style from his youth to his maturity, from Assisi to Padua. It was in the Florentine period, immediately following that of Assisi, that he executed the large *Crucifix* in Santa Maria Novella. Here the figure of Christ, abandoning the iconography used by Cimabue, the *Christus patiens* of medieval tradition, is represented in humanized form, with a beauty that is corporeal, for death is a prelude to the Resurrection. In comparison with the *Maestà* of Duccio and Cimabue, the majestic pose of the *Madonna and Child* painted for San Giorgio alla Costa and mentioned by Ghiberti has a naturalness and a solidity that refer to the *Madonnas* carved by Arnolfo di Cambio for the façade of Santa Maria del Fiore.

The fresco representing *Boniface VIII Taking Possession of the Lateran* in San Giovanni in Laterano, mutilated and now badly deteriorated, used to ornament the loggia built by the Caetani pope, who had commissioned it to affirm the legitimacy of his election.

During this second stay in Rome the Florentine painter assimilated and digested elements drawn from Roman antiquity and the results of this can be seen in all their complexity in the *Badia Polyptych* and the Paduan frescoes.

Alongside the ideas derived from antiquity, he was also influenced by the painting of Pietro Cavallini, with its pale and mellow colors, which he was able to admire in the cycles of paintings in Santa Maria in Trastevere (1291) and Santa Cecilia (1293).

Judging by the account of Riccobaldo Ferrarese, Giotto's presence in Rimini must date from before the Paduan period. The frescoes in San Francesco have been lost, but the influence he exercised on the painters of Rimini led to the formation of a school. In the folds of Christ's loincloth in the *Crucifix* in the Tempio Malatestiano, drawing still predominates over the use of color.

The Paduan Period. The Scrovegni Chapel

The Franciscan churches of Assisi, Rimini and Padua are the places mentioned by Riccobaldo Ferrarese around 1312 and the Codex Laurentius adds: "ac per ea quae pinxit in palatio comunis Padue." The representation of *Wrath*, one of the Vices painted by Giotto in the lower part of the Scrovegni Chapel, is cited by Francesco da Barberino in his *Commentari d'Amore*, written around 1310.

Ghiberti states that he "painted at Padua in the Friars Minor" and circa 1440 Michele Savonarola wrote: "Capitalumque Antoni nostri sic ornavit." The following century Marcantonio Michiel (*c.* 1550) declared: "the fresco of the Passion in the Chapter was by the hand of Giotto the Florentine." In 1550 Vasari attributed to Giotto the decoration of several chapels in the basilica of Sant'Antonio, but subsequently (1568) stated that he only painted one. So there are plenty of historical records to indicate that the activity of Giotto and his workshop in Padua was intense, carrying out commissions from both ecclesiastical and lay clients.

Giotto came to Padua at the invitation of the Franciscans, to decorate their chapterhouse and the chapel in the choir under the patronage of the Scrovegni family (Flores d'Arcais 1968). The frescoes have survived only in a fragmentary state, and have been repainted, but the conception, attributable to Giotto, and their execution by one of his close collaborators, whose hand can also be identified in the cycle of frescoes in the Scrovegni Chapel, date these works to some time prior to the decoration of Enrico Scrovegni's private chapel.

On January 6, 1300, Enrico bought a large area of land from the noble Paduan family of the Delesmanini on which to build his palace and chapel. Bishop Ortobono de Razzi authorized the construction of the chapel on April 29, 1302, and a year later, on March 25, 1303, a ceremony was held to mark the beginning of the work (Tolomei 1880 and 1884). The building was consecrated on March 25, 1305, with the vestments accorded by the Maggior Consiglio of Venice on March 16. The crosses set on the frame of the lower row of frescoes, many of which can still be seen today, were painted at the time of the chapel's consecration. The chapel, built in a short space of time and then sumptuously decorated, also had a campanile, whose bells were used to summon the faithful. For this reason the chapter of the Eremitani friars, whose church and monastery were located close to what was known as the area "of the Arena" owing to the presence of the ruins of the Roman amphitheater, lodged a formal protest with the bishop of Padua. Implicit in this, however, was the fact that the beauty of the decoration was likely to draw large numbers of worshipers at the expense of the nearby Eremitani church. In the area acquired by Enrico Scrovegni had stood, since at least 1278, a church where the feast day of the Annunciation was celebrated every March 25 with a solemn procession and a miracle play. It seems possible to discern a reflection of this performance in the architecture of two panels painted by Giotto on the triumphal arch of the chapel, depicting the *Announcing*

Angel and the *Annunciation*. The painting of *God the Father Instructing the Archangel Gabriel to Make the Announcement to Mary* on the wooden panel above would also seem to have the function of providing an opportunity to represent the Holy Spirit in the form of a dove, just as in the passion play of March 25.

The chapel consists of a single room measuring 20.5 by 8.5 meters and 18.5 meters high, roofed with a tunnel vault. A large archway opens onto the deep and narrow apse, illuminated by two tall windows with pointed arches. A large Gothic three-light window in the front and six tall Gothic single-light windows on the south side let light into the spacious interior. The architecture appears to have been designed to suit the needs of the painted decoration, and so it has been suggested that it was the work of Giotto himself (Gioseffi 1968). The original plan was for the chapel to have a transept, as it is shown in the model presented by Enrico Scrovegni to the Madonna on the inside of the front wall, but this was never built. The decoration of the apse, datable to between 1317 and 1320, also marks a break with the central space and the *Scenes of the Death of the Virgin* are the work of an anonymous follower of Giotto active in Padua, Lombardy and perhaps Friuli (Bologna 1969). It is likely that the change was made over the course of the work, as Giotto painted two perspective views alluding to the nonexistent transept on the lower part of the triumphal arch.

The decoration of the vault and walls follows a sequence starting from the top, with the starry sky in which are set tondi representing *Christ, Saint John the Baptist* and three *Prophets* in the part adjacent to the apsidal arch, and the *Madonna* and four *Prophets* in the part nearest to the façade. Two broad bands of decoration frame the archway and the façade, in which *Patriarchs, Prophets* and *Kings* of the Old Testament and *Apostles* and *Male* and *Female Saints* are represented half-length inside multifoil frames.

On the walls the narration unfolds in scenes arranged in three tiers. Starting at the top of the right-hand wall, these depict *Scenes from the Lives of Saints Joachim and Anne* and *Scenes from the Life of Mary*, based on the stories in the Apocrypha. They are followed by *Scenes from the Childhood, Passion and Death of Christ*, drawn from the accounts in the Gospels. On the north wall they are separated by decorative bands in which episodes from the Old Testament "prefiguring" those of the New Testament (Bellinati 1975 and 1997) are represented inside mixtilinear frames.

The *Last Judgment* is depicted on the west wall. Linked with it are the *Virtues* and *Vices*, figures painted in monochrome in imitation of marble reliefs on the lower part of the side walls. They are intended to show that virtue, or its counterposed vice, leads the human being to Heaven or to Hell.

Giotto, drawing on his recent stay in Rome, painted this lower zone with a tall base of variegated marble panels and niches in which the allegories of *Virtues* and *Vices* are set like marble sculptures. From this base rise the frames that separate the various scenes and the three bands of the ceiling. The representation of space grows even more evident in the individual scenes, where the figures are inserted in settings that are disposed at a slight angle.

The space is systematically foreshortened, as are the faces. These, depicted side-on or from below, as in the soldiers of the *Resurrection*, produce effects of surprising modernity. The emotions of the figures and the sense of unfolding drama are conveyed through the intensity of the gazes, the gestures of the hands and bodies.

Giotto experiments with the quality of the light and thus the frescoes are painted in layers of glaze, so as to create transparences, colored shadows, subtle nuances of shade, iridescences and unexpected shifts of tone. Settings, vestments, furnishings and landscapes are intended to be realistic representations of daily life, in order to show the relevance of the Gospel account to the present.

This makes the images an indirect record of the uses and customs of a rich and powerful society, and an explicit celebration of the power of Enrico Scrovegni himself, who was attempting to establish political control over Padua. He would not succeed in realizing his ambitions, but it is evident that the decoration of the chapel of his palace was intended to remind the citizenry of the ducal chapel of the rulers of Venice. Enrico would go into exile in Venice in 1320, but in his will asked to be buried in his chapel, which duly happened on November 23, 1336.

The altar was adorned with sculptures by Giovanni Pisano, among the most refined and elegant products of the Italian Gothic.

In his *Vita Aegidii Regis Patavi* (1340-50), Giovanni da Nono describes the ancient king Aegidius's vision of the future city of Padua. In the description it is said that Giotto would decorate the Palazzo della Ragione, hub of public life in Padua, with twelve signs of the Zodiac, seven Planets and their "properties." According to Paduan tradition, commencing with Michele Savonarola, the iconography was inspired by Petrus de Abano's treatise on astrology *Lucidator* and illustrated the influence of the heavenly bodies on the works and temperaments of men. The decoration, lost forever in the fire of 1420, was reproduced in the cycle of paintings by Giovanni

Miretto and an anonymous Ferrarese painter (1420-35), which presumably adopted the same iconography. Giotto's influence in Padua, Verona, Trent and Friuli derives entirely from the stylistic characteristics of his work during the first decade of the 14th century, before he painted the Peruzzi Chapel, and so the decoration of the hall in the Palazzo della Ragione must also have been completed by the end of that decade.

The Works after Padua: Assisi, Florence, Rome, Naples, Milan

The role played by Giotto's collaborators within his workshop, wholly under the master's control and displaying an extraordinary uniformity of style in the cycle of frescoes in the Scrovegni Chapel, is more evident in the pictures painted in Assisi, before and after the Paduan period.

Returning to Florence, Giotto executed a *Maestà* for the church of Ognissanti, now in the Uffizi. Its composition and color make it one of his finest works. In comparison with the frescoes in Padua, here he made more use of chiaroscuro than outline to define the volumes of the faces. He also painted the altar frontal with the *Dormitio Virginis* for the church of Ognissanti, while a close collaborator, known as "Giotto's Relative," executed the large *Crucifix*.

We know him to have been in Rome in 1313, working on the cartoon for a large mosaic in the loggia of St. Peter's basilica. The mosaic has vanished, apart from two fragments with *Angels*.

Ghiberti and Vasari record four chapels and four polyptychs in the Florentine church of Santa Croce executed to commissions from wealthy and influential bourgeois families. Of the four chapels cited in the sources, only two, the Peruzzi and Bardi Chapels, have been preserved. Their dating is a problem much debated by the critics.

Painted in an even larger and more unitary space with respect to the observer than in Padua, the frescoes in the Peruzzi Chapel are in fact a continuation of Giotto's experimentation with "perspective" in the Scrovegni Chapel. They enjoyed great fame, and Michelangelo copied some of the figures. The cycle of paintings, in fresco with large areas finished in tempera, attest to Giotto's willingness to try out new techniques of execution in order to develop new forms of expression.

He also painted the polyptych now in the Gemäldegalerie at Dresden, presumably at around the same time as the cycle of frescoes, 1314-15.

Giotto's presence in the chapel of the Magdalen at Assisi is a recent discovery by the critics and still the subject of much debate (Gnudi

1957). The episodes from the life of Mary Magdalene drawn from Jacobus de Voragine's *Golden Legend* are set in sweeping landscapes where nature predominates over the figures. Giotto was assisted by the "Master of the Vaulting Cells," who was responsible for the decoration of the cross vault of the transept of the lower church of San Francesco with representations of the Franciscan virtues of *Poverty*, *Chastity* and *Obedience* and with the *Glory of the Saint*. The same collaborator worked with Giotto on the polyptych for Cardinal Jacopo Stefaneschi, formerly on the high altar of the basilica of St. Peter and now in the Pinacoteca Vaticana, dated to 1320. Before Giotto's departure for Naples in 1328, he decorated the Bardi Chapel with *Scenes from the Life of Saint Francis* and painted the Baroncelli Polyptych. From 1328 to 1333 Giotto and his assistants worked for the Angevins in Naples and, appointed court painter in 1330, was promoted to "familiar" (member of the royal household). This new and profoundly different social status brought him into contact with the literary and humanist circles, including many Florentines, that surrounded King Robert. The works he realized in Naples, recorded by the local sources, have almost all been lost. The most unusual of them, in that it belonged to the medieval tradition but had been updated to suit the pre-humanistic climate of the Neapolitan court, was the decoration of the palace's Magna Sala with *Illustrious Men*, a cycle of paintings from which Petrarch may have taken the inspiration for his *De Viris Illustribus*.

In 1334 Giotto, back in Florence, was appointed *Magister et gubernator* of the Vestry Board of Santa Reparata, as well as architect of the city's walls and fortifications. From there he went to the court of Azzone Visconti in Milan and, according to Ghiberti, painted a *Vana Gloria* in the palace. Galvano Fiamma (1342) lists the illustrious men of antiquity represented in this work, alongside whom there were also portraits of Charlemagne and Azzone Visconti.

Returning from Milan to Florence, he died on January 18, 1337.

The Scrovegni Chapel

Legend

1. The Eternal
A, B. Tribunes
2. The Expulsion
of Joachim from
the Temple
3. Joachim among
the Shepherds
4. Annunciation of
the Angel to Anne
5. The Sacrifice
of Joachim
6. Joachim's Dream
7. The Meeting
Between Joachim
and Anne at the
Golden Gate
8. The Birth of Mary
9. The Presentation
of Mary in the
Temple
10. The Rods Brought
to the Temple
11. The Prayers
of Joseph and
the Other Suitors
in the Temple
12. The Marriage of
Mary and Joseph
13. The Wedding
Procession of Mary

14 a, b. God the
Father Instructing
the Archangel
Gabriel to Make
the Announcement
to Mary.
The Annunciation
15. The Visitation
of Mary to Elizabeth
16. The Nativity
of Jesus
17. The Adoration
of the Magi
18. The Presentation
of Jesus in the
Temple
19. The Flight
into Egypt
20. The Slaughter
of the Innocents
21. Christ among
the Doctors in the
Temple
22. The Baptism
of Christ
23. The Marriage
at Cana
24. The Raising
of Lazarus
25. Christ's Entry
into Jerusalem

26. Christ Driving
the Moneychangers
from the Temple
27. The Betrayal
of Judas
28. The Last Supper
29. The Washing
of Feet
30. The Kiss of Judas
31. Christ before
Caiaphas
32. Christ Mocked
33. The Road to
Calvary
34. The Crucifixion
35. Lamentation
over the Dead Christ
36. Noli me tangere.
The Resurrection of
Christ
37. The Ascension
38. Pentecost
39. The Last
Judgment
40 a-g. Virtues
41 a-g. Vices
42, 43. The Vault
and the Decorative
Bands

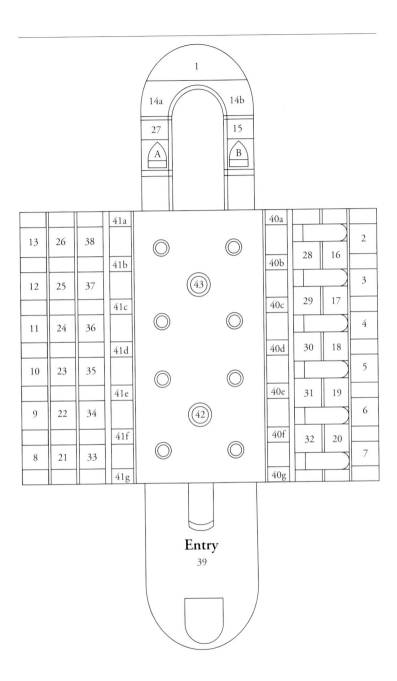

Entry

39

The Frescoes

Anna Maria Spiazzi

The Expulsion of Joachim from the Temple (2)

It is told in the apocryphal Gospels that Joachim, who had gone to the temple to offer the sacrificial lamb, was expelled by the scribe Ruben: "It is not lawful for thee to stand among those who are doing sacrifice to God, because God has not blessed thee so as to give thee seed in Israel" (Pseudo Matthew, 2:1). The ciborium and the pulpit, or *bimah* for the Jews, are represented architecturally in a manner analogous to the *sancta sanctorum* of the early Christian basilicas, which Giotto had seen in Rome and reproduced here, though updated to reflect the "modern" style of Arnolfo di Cambio.

Joachim among the Shepherds (3)

Joachim "went to his flocks, taking with him his shepherds into the mountains to a far country, so that for five months his wife Anne could hear no tidings of him." Joachim's suffering is conveyed through his attitude, with head bowed. In contrast, the shepherds' little dog runs up to greet him with affectionate vivacity.

The clear expression of the figures' feelings is matched by the construction of their volumes, reduced to the essential to leave room for the wooded and mountainous landscape. In this scene and the following ones, the attention paid to nature, already apparent in the episodes represented at Assisi, becomes the dominant element.

Annunciation of the Angel to Anne (4)

Anne, praying in her room, receives the announcement from the angel, who tells her: "Be not afraid, Anne, for there is seed for thee in the decree of God." Anne's room is given classical forms with a tympanum, on which two winged putti hold the bust of a man, the

The Last Judgment (39), detail

prophet Isaiah, framed in a shell (Bellinati 1997). Inside the room, the furnishings are those typical of the 14th century: trunk, bench, bed with a striped blanket. The sanctity of the event is conveyed through the image of Anne kneeling in prayer, but its credibility is entrusted to the angel, whose foreshortened figure occupies the whole space of the window at which he appears.

The Sacrifice of Joachim (5)

The angel announces to Joachim that Anne will give birth. "And when Joachim was offering the sacrifice to God, the angel and the odor of the sacrifice went together straight up to heaven with the smoke." The skeleton of the sacrificial lamb is represented on the altar and above it, as an allegory of Joachim's prayer rising to heaven, Giotto has sketched the outline of a head in profile. Above the allegory of prayer we see the hand of God, blessing and welcoming it. The carefully drawn and painted flowers anticipate, by a long time, the illuminated pages of the "herbals" produced in Padua at the end of the 14th century for scientific and naturalistic purposes. It is a new way of perceiving nature and enjoying it in all its splendor, with observations made from life.

Joachim's Dream (6)

Joachim receives the angel's message in a dream: "go down with confidence, and return to Anne." The mystical vision has its emotional core in the sleeping figure of Joachim, huddled in on itself to form the geometric shape of a pyramid. The action, i.e. the angel, the shepherds and the sheep, is shifted as far as possible to the left, so that the space is left empty in the middle. The shepherd leaning on his staff in the foreground and the figure of Joachim, often compared to the sculptures of Nicola Pisano and Arnolfo di Cambio, are among the finest pieces of Italian painting of all time.

The Meeting Between Joachim and Anne at the Golden Gate (7)

Joachim meets Anne at the gate of Jerusalem: "she ran to him and hung on his neck, giving thanks to God."

The kiss as an act symbolizing procreation, of classical origin, lasted with different nuances of meaning into the Middle Ages. The archway of the city gate, apparently based on the Roman arch in Rimini, may constitute indirect evidence of Giotto's activity in that city prior to 1305.

The woman with her face partially covered is either a symbol of the Synagogue or an allusion to Anne's widowhood in the past. The young

women watching the joyful encounter have their hair gathered into elegant braids and are lively portraits rather than stereotyped figures.

The Meeting Between Joachim and Anne at the Golden Gate (7)

The Birth of Mary (8)

To illustrate the unity of the location of the events narrated Giotto represents Anne's house exactly as it had appeared in the *Annunciation of the Angel to Anne* (4). And to emphasize the depth of the room he depicts the rectangle of the poles from which the drapes hang in "perspective." In the space geometrically defined in this way he places two beautiful female figures, one holding dishes with food and the other proffering the newborn Mary, wrapped in swaddling clothes, to Anne. This woman, in a blue dress with gold borders, appears to be of high social class and we can speculate that the figure is a portrait of Enrico Scrovegni's wife, especially in view of the fact that in his frescoes in Padua Baptistery Giusto de' Menabuoi repre-

The Birth of Mary (8)

sents his client, Fina Buzzacarini, and her daughters paying homage to St. Elizabeth in the scene of the *Birth of John the Baptist.*

The Presentation of Mary in the Temple (9)

Anne and Joachim "went together to the temple of the Lord to offer sacrifices to God, and placed the infant, Mary by name, in the community of virgins, in which the virgins remained day and night praising God." The temple becomes the architectural space that determines, by diagonals, the location of the figures: the priest in the middle, with Mary, two more priests at bottom right and St. Anne and the youth with a basket on the left. The scene acquires depth and everything is dominated by the imposing figure of Anne, whose cloak spreads out in a great patch of color. The panels of mottled marble and the slender columns are a reflection of Roman architecture, filtered through the style of Arnolfo di Cambio.

The Presentation of Mary in the Temple (9)

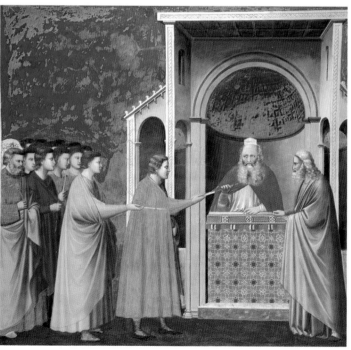

The Rods Brought to the Temple (10)

The Prayers of Joseph and the Other Suitors in the Temple (11)

The Marriage of Mary and Joseph (12)

The Rods Brought to the Temple (10)

The young men bring the rods to the priest, as Abiathar had said he had been commanded by God: "Put all their rods into the holy of holies [...]." The temple is a building with a single nave with a flat ceiling and two aisles. The apsidal conch has a geometric decoration depicted in "perspective," reflecting Giotto's continuing experimentation with the representation of three dimensions. The altar frontal, adorned with a piece of cloth with a geometrical pattern, alludes to the precious fabrics of the 14th century and to the courtly refinement of the setting.

The Prayers of Joseph and the Other Suitors in the Temple (11)

The priest and the young men gather in prayer as they wait for a sign from God. The rods are placed on top of the altar, along with two sacred vessels. The strain of waiting can be read in the gazes, all fixed on the altar, in the marked profiles and in the arched backs of the kneeling figures. Joseph, located almost out of the field of view, a foreshortened figure in the background, becomes the most fervent expression of the anxious wait, which is described as follows in the Apocrypha: "[...] Joseph remained apart, in a corner."

The Marriage of Mary and Joseph (12)

Mary is handed over to Joseph, in accordance with the will of God, and the wedding ceremony is held in a temple, represented in the same way as in the preceding scenes. The group of young men on the left creates a continuity with the previous episode and one of them is shown in the act of breaking his rod over his knee. The slender figure of the young maiden Mary is given a Gothic intonation by the long train of her white dress. The hand resting on her belly seems to allude in a natural manner to her maternity, while Joseph places the ring on her finger.

The Wedding Procession of Mary (13)

The supple elegance of Mary and the girls in her procession has led some critics to hypothesize a visit to France by Giotto, although there is no documentary evidence for this. In fact it is easy to explain Giotto's Gothicism by the influence of Giovanni Pisano's sculptures and the echoes of French style that may have arrived in Italy in the form of small ivory carvings, illuminations and enamels applied to church ornaments and profane objects. The perfect balance between naturalness and idealization in the group of three youths with clarions and a vielle makes it one of the finest bits of painting in the

whole Paduan cycle. Giotto would use a variant of the young man with puffed cheeks again for one of the angels in the *Dormitio Virginis*, painted as an altar frontal for Ognissanti in Florence and now in Berlin. The panel has been badly damaged by the seepage of damp, already recorded graphically in the last century, and by the opening of a window in the 16th century to allow the Scrovegni family to watch services held in the chapel from above.

God the Father Instructing the Archangel Gabriel to Make the Announcement to Mary. The Annunciation (1 and 14 a, b)

The whole of the lunette of the triumphal arch is taken up by the first part of the episode. The throne on which God the Father is seated stands on a tall podium, with three steps, in Cosmatesque marble with lion heads. The articulation of the three polygonal bases is scaled in "perspective," making the semicircular space of the two arrays of angels measurable. The angels are also scaled in depth and advance and recede

*God the Father
Instructing the
Archangel Gabriel
to Make the
Announcement
to Mary.
The Annunciation
(1, 14 a, b), details*

alternately in relation to the space they occupy. Their gazes and gestures create an intense animation. Another beautiful element is the group of angels with a portative organ, vielle and flutes, an iconographic theme that was to be developed in 14th- and 15th-century painting, especially in the *Paradise* on the large dome of the baptistery in Padua.

God the Father is addressing the Archangel Gabriel, standing on his right, and it is a beautiful image despite the fact that the painting, executed on a wooden panel, has suffered grave damage.

The *Annunciation* marks the beginning of the narration based on the text of the Gospels: "And in the sixth month the angel Gabriel was sent from God unto a city of Galilee, named Nazareth, to a virgin espoused to a man whose name was Joseph, of the house of David; and the virgin's name was Mary" (Luke, 1:26-7). The Announcing Angel and the Virgin Mary, at the sides of the arch and kneeling one in front of the other, are inserted in two identical and spacious archi-

tectural recesses, each with a loggetta and a coffered ceiling. It has been suggested that these two structures are a memory of the aedicules used for the miracle play that used to be staged on March 25, first in the cathedral and then in the "arena," where an oratory dedicated to Our Lady of the Annunciation had stood since 1278.

The Nativity of Jesus (16), detail

The Visitation of Mary to Elizabeth (15)

"And Mary arose in those days, and went into the hill country with haste, into a city of Judas; and entered into the house of Zacharias, and saluted Elizabeth" (Luke, 1:39-40). Elizabeth, the mother of St. John the Baptist, recognizes Mary as the mother of the Savior long awaited by the Jewish people. The use of patterns, perhaps on cartoons as has been proposed for the frescoes in San Francesco at Assisi (Zanardi, Zeri, Frugoni 1996), may well have been the practice in Padua as well: the repetition of iconographic models necessarily requires some physiognomic consistency. The almost total loss of the blue pigment from the dress of the woman on the right allows the preparatory drawing to show through and thus reveals the technique used by Giotto in this stylistic phase.

The Nativity of Jesus (16)

"Mary [...] placed the child in the stall, and the ox and the ass adored Him" (Pseudo Matthew, 14:1).

The foreshortening used for the ass constitutes one of the greatest innovations in Italian painting. The two shepherds, holding a dialogue with the angel at the top to emphasize the unity of time and action and thus of participation in the episode depicted, are also foreshortened, from behind. The iconography, of Byzantine origin and recurrent in the Middle Ages, has been profoundly renewed through the representation of human emotions. The squatting figure of Joseph and the standing ones of the two shepherds were to be used as models many times by Giotto's collaborators and can be found in particular in the scene of the same subject in the right transept at Assisi.

The Adoration of the Magi (17)

"Magi came from the east to Jerusalem, bringing great gifts. [...] And while the magi were going on their way, there appeared to them the star, which was, as it were, a guide to them, going before them until they came to where the child was. And [...] going into the house, they saw the child Jesus sitting in His mother's lap. Then they opened their treasures, and presented great gifts [...]. And likewise one gave gold, another frankincense, and the third myrrh" (Pseudo Matthew, 16). The angel on Mary's right is wearing a loose and flowing robe; the sleeves are tight at the cuffs and wide at the elbow, as was the fashion in the early 14th century. The loss of the paint, laid on *a secco*, from the wooden upright of the stable allows us to see the face of the angel behind Mary. Most of the azurite of the cloak has also worn away, revealing the preparatory drawing.

The Presentation of Jesus in the Temple (18)

"Symeon [...] took Him up into his cloak and kissed His feet, and said: Lord, now lettest Thou Thy servant depart in peace, according to Thy word. There was also in the temple of the Lord, Anna, a prophetess [...]. She also likewise adored the child, saying: In Him is the redemption of the world" (Pseudo Matthew, 15:6-7). These last words are inscribed on the scroll: "Quoniam in isto erit redemptio mundi." The fact that this sentence only appears in the Gospel according to the Pseudo Matthew provides indirect confirmation of the iconographic source (Bellinati 1997).

The composition proved extremely popular among not just Giotto's followers but other artists throughout the 14th century. In particular it was repeated by the goldsmith Francesco da Milano in 1375 on the tomb of St. Simeon in Zadar.

The Flight into Egypt (19)

An angel appears to Joseph and tells him to flee with Mary and the Child to Egypt. "And Joseph went according to the saying of the angel. [...] And there were with Joseph three boys, and with Mary a girl, going on the journey along with them" (Pseudo Matthew, 17 and 18). The scene, one of the most famous in the cycle, is wholly comprised within the pyramid geometrically defined by the rock at the center in the background. On the central axis of this geometrical-spatial definition, Mary and the Child also form a pyramidal composition. The drama of the sacred story and the gracefulness of the narration are perfectly balanced. The mountain scenery and the trees are painted in pale or dark tones depending on whether they are in the shade or the light.

The Slaughter of the Innocents (20)

Having failed to capture the Magi, Herod sends soldiers to Bethlehem to kill all children less than two years old. King Herod watches the slaughter of the children from a loggia. The temple on an octagonal plan on the right, perhaps a representation of the church of San Francesco in Bologna, is a symbolic allusion to the martyrdom and cult of the Holy Innocents. In fact the discovery of relics connected with the Holy Innocents in the Paduan basilica of Santa Giustina (1053) had led to the development of a cult that was particularly important in the city during the Middle Ages.

Christ among the Doctors in the Temple (21)

After looking for Jesus for three days, Mary and Joseph find him seated among the Doctors in the temple in Jerusalem, listening to them and asking them questions. "And when they saw him, they were amazed: and his mother said unto him, Son, why hast thou thus dealt with us? behold, thy father and I have sought thee sorrowing. And he said unto them, How is it that ye sought me? wist ye not that I must be about my Father's business?" (Luke, 2:48-9). The doctors are arrayed at the sides, leaving empty the central part where Jesus is seated, in harmony with the void behind the apsidal conch, which lends depth to the scene. The badly deteriorated panel was detached in the 19th century and has been abraded in many places, so that much of the coat of paint has been lost.

The Baptism of Christ (22)

While Jesus, immersed in the waters of the River Jordan, is baptized by John the Baptist, " [...] the heaven was opened, and the Holy Ghost descended in a bodily shape like a dove upon him, and a voice came from heaven, which said, Thou art my beloved Son; in thee I am well pleased" (Luke, 3:21-2). The Eternal Father, at the top and in line with Christ, extends his right hand in blessing and holds the book of Holy Scriptures in his left. The transparence of the river water leaves visible Jesus's body and even the fish swimming by his legs. The two rocky wings define the funnel-shaped space in which the figure of Christ is set. The very carefully executed preparatory drawing of the figure on the right, a disciple of the Baptist, is visible because the blue pigment has almost completely vanished.

The Marriage at Cana (23)

"Jesus saith unto them, Fill the waterpots with water [...], and bear unto the governor of the feast. [...] When [he] had tasted the water that was made wine, the governor of the feast called the bridegroom, and saith unto him, [...] thou hast kept the good wine until now."

41

The Marriage at Cana (23), details

(John, 2:7-10). Giotto depicts the moment when the governor of the feast tastes the wine in a very lively fashion, creating one of the most realistic and most imitated figures in 14th-century painting. Another figure of great beauty is the woman viewed from the back who is pouring water from a jug into the jars, here given the form of classical amphorae. Giotto's constant investigation of the geometricization of forms is especially evident in these syntheses of volumes, which capture the bodies in movement from particular angles.

The Raising of Lazarus (24), detail

The richly adorned dress of the bride, wearing a crown on her head, the tablecloth, the fabric covering the walls of the room, the amphora on the loggia at the top and the dishes and drinking glasses provide a record of life in the 14th century.

The Raising of Lazarus (24)

Coming to the grave where Lazarus has been buried, Jesus asks for the stone that covers its opening to be removed and calls to Lazarus: "And he that was dead came forth, bound hand and foot with grave-clothes: and his face was bound about with a napkin. Jesus saith unto them, Loose him, and let him go" (John, 11:44).

The miraculous event, to which the disciples react with amazement and Lazarus's sisters Martha and Mary with devotion, kneeling at Christ's feet, is emblematically summed up in the face of the man returned from the dead, his eyes and mouth half-closed. The putrefaction of his body is conveyed by the gesture of the disciple on the right, who covers his nose with his cloak: a figure that Giusto de' Menabuoi would imitate in his depiction of the same scene in the cycle of frescoes in the baptistery.

Christ's Entry into Jerusalem (25)

"And the disciples went, and did as Jesus commanded them, and brought the ass, and the colt, and put on them their clothes, and they set him thereon. And a very great multitude spread their garments in the way; others cut down branches from the trees, and strewed them in the way" (Matthew, 21:6-8). The realistic annotations in this scene are vividly expressed in the man on the right, who is about to take off his tunic, and, in a humorous tone, in the young man with his head and arms still caught in his clothing. The ass and colt are depicted with great efficacy, with detailed attention paid to representing the gray and white hairs of the ass's muzzle with fine lines.

Christ Driving the Moneychangers from the Temple (26)

"And Jesus went into the temple of God, and cast out all them that

sold and bought in the temple, and overthrew the tables of the moneychangers, and the seats of them that sold doves" (Matthew, 21:12). The overturned table, painted partly *a secco* and partly in fresco, is represented in "perspective," as is the façade of the temple. The tympana of the porch, with round arches, are in a classical style and the two horses in the middle may be an allusion to the ones on the front of St. Mark's basilica in Venice. Christ's angry gesture contrasts with the affectionate attitude of the child holding the dove. John's pose is intensely expressive, as he uses his left hand to cover his bowed head with his cloak and draws the frightened little girl to him with his right.

The Betrayal of Judas (27)
"Then entered Satan into Judas surnamed Iscariot, being of the number of the twelve. And he went his way, and communed with the chief priests and captains, how he might betray him unto them. And they were glad, and covenanted to give him money" (Luke, 22:3-5). The representation of Satan as a devil was common in the Middle Ages and in popular tradition, and is an iconographic motif that Giotto used in the *Last Judgment* as well.

The Last Supper (28)
Jesus announces that one of his disciples will betray him, and John, "lying on Jesus' breast saith unto him, Lord, who is it? Jesus answered, He it is, to whom I shall give a sop, when I have dipped it" (John, 13:25-6). Judas, seated in the corner on the left, is about to receive the sign of recognition from Christ. The other apostles are seated around the laid table, five of them viewed from the front and five in the foreground, sitting on the bench with their backs to us and set at a slight angle to the lower edge of the panel. This minor shift in "perspective" is matched at the top by the angle of the roof and ceiling. Full light plays over the colors of the clothes of the figures in the foreground, while those of the ones seated against the back wall are painted in darker tones. The robe of the apostle in the middle, adorned with a minute gold decoration, is the point of greatest luminosity.

The Washing of Feet (29)
Jesus washes and dries the feet of the apostles. "Then cometh he to Simon Peter: and Peter saith unto him, Lord, dost thou wash my feet?" (John, 13:6). Christ and Peter constitute the fulcrum of the composition and exchange intense glances. The figure of St. John holding the jug is constructed as if it had been carved out of a block of marble and is reminiscent, in its monumentality, of the sculptures of Arnolfo di

Cambio. The unity of space and time with the previous scene is conveyed by the use of the same architectural setting.

The Kiss of Judas (30)

Judas embraces and kisses Jesus, identifying him to the soldiers who have
come to arrest him. "Then Simon Peter having a sword drew it, and
smote the high priest's servant, and cut off his right ear. The servant's
name was Malchus" (John, 18:10). The bloody act is depicted with great
realism. The threat represented by the soldiers, crowded behind the central block of the figures of Christ and Judas, is rendered by the bristling
of helmets, spears and torches against the backdrop of the night sky. The
faces, also portrayed with marked realism, convey a sense of aggressive-
ness and guilt through the irregularity of their features.

Christ before Caiaphas (31)

Interrogated by the priests, Jesus answers them: "I spake openly to the
world [...]." Immediately one of the guards strikes Jesus, saying "Answer-
est thou the high priest so?" (John, 18:20 and 22).
The soldier on the left has his hand raised to strike Jesus and Caiaphas
is rending his clothes. As the sacred drama proceeds the gestures grow

more and more explicit and emotionally charged. The faces become sullen and the features increasingly marked. The ostentatious realism of Caiaphas's gesture speaks louder than words, as does the figure of Christ, his gaze intense but his suffering conveyed through the slight curve of his shoulders.

Christ Mocked (32)

The priests and Pilate look on as Christ is mocked by the soldiers, who "bowed the knee before him, and mocked him, saying, Hail, King of the Jews!" (Matthew, 27:29). The scene is set in a courtyard of the palace. Elegant columns support the entablature decorated with palmettes and lions in a classicizing style, based on Roman models. The faces of Pilate and the man on his right, perhaps a soldier, are depicted in such a naturalistic manner that they seem to be actual portraits. In this scene the experimentation with the representation of forms by colored masses bathed in light produces one of the most perfect results in the whole cycle of paintings.

The Road to Calvary (33)

Christ, bent under the weight of the great cross, staggers toward Cal-

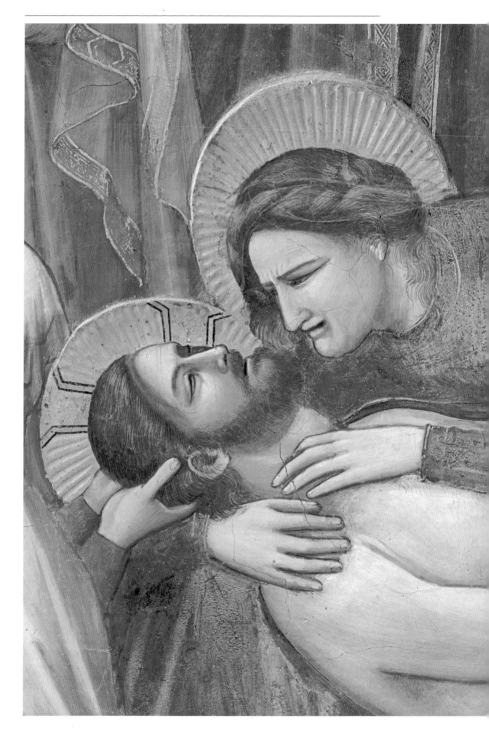

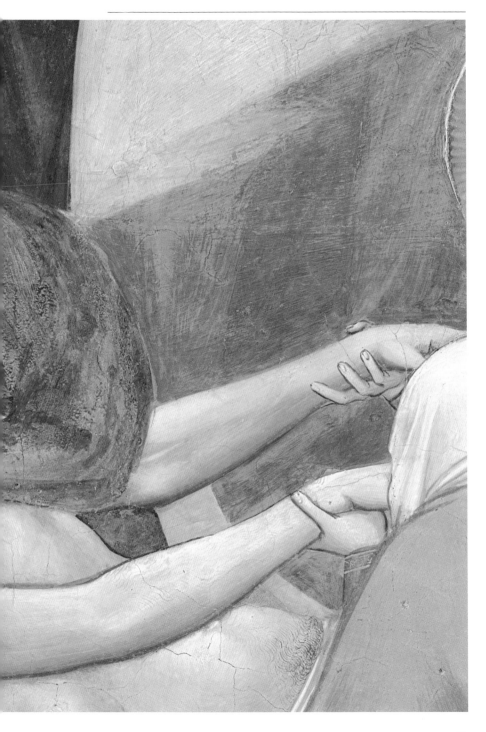

Lamentation over the Dead Christ (35)

On preceding pages, *Lamentation over the Dead Christ* (35), detail

vary but turns to look at his mother, who is pushed back by a soldier. It is one of the most intense images in Italian painting. A sense of physical space and of powerful emotions is communicated by the gazes of the protagonists of the drama, which is human as well as sacred. The sculptural blocks formed by the figures of Christ and Mary constitute the two main pivots of the composition.

The Crucifixion (34)

Angels fly around the cross making gestures of despair, rending their garments and throwing back their arms, while three of them collect the blood flowing from his side and hands. The "Most Precious Blood of Christ" was one of the most venerated relics in the Middle Ages. It was kept in a reliquary in the Treasury of St. Mark's in Venice, having been brought there from Constantinople. The angels are represented in foreshortened views, from below or the side, in order to convey the impression that they are hovering in the air around the cross. The conception of the image is extremely beautiful, as is its execution. Christ's body is modeled with glazes laid on in a very liquid state. The centurion is depicted with a halo as in the Middle Ages he was considered a saint.

Facing page, *Noli me tangere. The Resurrection of Christ* (36), detail

Lamentation over the Dead Christ (35)

Joseph of Arimathea and Nicodemus obtain permission from Pilate to carry away Jesus's body and bury it in a tomb. The scene of the *Lamentation over the Dead Christ*, an iconographic theme that was popular in medieval literature too, for instance in the Laud of Jacopone da Todi, is one of the most dramatic and expressive of the panels.

The juxtaposition of the faces of Christ and his mother, one stiffened in death and the other with grief, communicates a pathos of great emotional force. The two seated women viewed from behind, one with her hands raised to support Christ's head and the other holding his right hand, Mary Magdalene also seated on the ground and clasping his right foot, St. John and the group of the three Marys standing on the left are all united in Mary's sorrow, as in a laud.

The scene was used as a model of composition and form throughout the 14th century.

Noli me tangere. The Resurrection of Christ (36)

Mary Magdalene goes to Christ's sepulcher and finds two angels there, who say to her: "Woman, why weepest thou? She saith unto them, Because they have taken away my Lord, and I know not where they have laid him. [...] Jesus saith unto her, Mary. She turned herself, and saith unto him, Rabboni; which is to say, Master" (John, 20:13-16).

The two moments are represented in a single scene and again it is the rock in the background, in diagonal, that guides the gaze toward the figure of Christ on the right, who is about to exit from the scene, as if in a passion play, and who is holding the banner of resurrection, inscribed with the words "VICTOR MORTIS." The scene is rich in figurative elements that were repeated in subsequent 14th-century painting. The figures of the sleeping soldiers would long be imitated for the beautiful way in which Giotto has conceived their foreshortening and depicted the features of their faces with just a few lines.

The Ascension (37)

"And when he had spoken these things, while they beheld, he was taken up; and a cloud received him out of their sight" (Acts of the Apostles, 1:9).

The light given off by Christ is so bright that the Apostles have to screen their eyes to watch the miraculous event. Two hosts of angels and Old Testament prophets accompany Christ in his ascent and are depicted alternately from the front and in profile, to lend depth and articulation to the space. The clothes of the angels are decorated with gold embroidery in a geometric-floral style.

56

Pentecost (38)

"And when the day of Pentecost was fully come, they were all with one accord in one place [...] and they were all filled with the Holy Ghost, and began to speak with other tongues, as the Spirit gave them utterance" (Acts of the Apostles, 2:1-4). To their profound astonishment the Spirit radiates to the Apostles in the form of tongues of fire, causing them to look up or to question one another. In this last panel Giotto's research into "perspective" takes another step forward. The figures seen from behind, in the foreground, are given broad and strong volumes, like sculptural blocks of color and light. In contrast, the clothing of the Apostles seated on the bench against the rear wall is densely shaded to bring out the different tones of the colors in relation to the different amounts of light absorbed. Optical experimentation, based on real observation, is transferred into painting and these are the first reflections that would lead Giotto to try out, as Vasari put it, a "molten and very even" painting.

The Tribunes (A and B)

On the lower part of the triumphal arch Giotto painted two mock works

of architecture, two spaces bounded by a pointed arch in the foreground, Gothic two-light windows in the back wall and strongly foreshortened cross vaults. In each a metal lamp hanging from the middle of the ceiling renders the painted structures credible (Toesca 1941, Longhi 1952). The novelty of such a precociously "Renaissance" handling of perspective has been linked to the hypothesis of Giotto's involvement in the architectural design of the Scrovegni Chapel. Indirect evidence for this is thought to come from the model of the chapel with a transept that Enrico presents to the Madonna in the *Last Judgment* painted on the inside of the front wall. The structures, or tribunes, have been interpreted as the mortuary chapels of Enrico and his father Reginaldo.

The Last Judgment (39)

On the west wall, illuminated by the large Gothic three-light window which was probably designed by Giotto, is set the *Last Judgment*, one of the most popular iconographic themes of the Middle Ages.

In this scene too Giotto's compositional skills find expression in a geometric definition of the space. Christ is supported by the symbols of the four Evangelists: the eagle (St. John), the bull (St. Luke), the angel (St. Matthew) and the lion (St. Mark). He is surrounded by a nimbus symbolizing the heavens, supported by cherubim and seraphim. According to the vision of the Apocalypse, the gates of heaven are opened, and they are represented here by two angels, gates studded with gems and the sun and the moon. Christ the Judge, flanked by hosts of angels and the twelve Apostles, calls to him, with his right hand turned downward, the host of the Saints and the Blessed, led by Mary, *Regina coelorum*, and the host underneath, guided by angels, of the People of God, of the Church, who have earned Paradise. With his left hand, he dismisses the reprobates. From the nimbus of the heavens in which Christ is seated flows a river of fire that splits into four branches and engulfs the damned, divided into three groups, one for each of three deadly sins: Covetousness, Lust and Pride. At the bottom of the infernal abyss Lucifer torments the damned for eternity while on the side of Christ's right hand the dead rise to eternal bliss. Underneath Christ the Judge two angels hold the cross, separating Hell from Heaven. On the right of the cross, again from the viewpoint of Christ, Enrico Scrovegni kneels in devotion and offers a model of the chapel to the Madonna, who shows her acceptance of the gift by holding out her right hand to him. On Mary's right stands St. John, on her left St. Catherine, the saints to whom the two altars in the middle section of the chapel are dedicated. The model is supported by Altegrado de' Cattanei, canon and archpriest of the cathedral and friend of Enrico Scrovegni.

In this scene too, despite the complexity of the iconography and composition, Giotto makes experiments with design, color and light that prove highly effective. Although the angels in the host are divided into groups, their heads are turned to one side or the other, thereby avoiding the flattening effect of a frontal view. This results in a variety of gazes, foreshortenings and expressions that are never repetitive and produce an idealized gallery of portraits. Even though located very high up, Christ's face has been depicted with extraordinary skill, using superimposed coats of paint ranging from pink to white to render it luminous. The technique of painting developed by Giotto in Padua allowed him to arrive, through a series of experiments, at the physiognomic depiction of his figures' faces, differentiating them and thus making them highly realistic. The Apostles have features that render them recognizable, even in different scenes, and among the ranks of the Saints and the Blessed there are also faces that are characterized as portraits. One genuine portrait is that of Enrico Scrovegni, presented here for the first time life size, i.e. on the same scale as the Madonna and the Saints.

Hell is depicted through images of great realism and the representation of the figures of devils, in gray and black, and of the damned, in red and brown, with broad and confident brushstrokes is remarkable. While the contribution made by the workshop in these parts is considered to have been fairly extensive, there are elements which are so unprecedented and innovative that the constant supervision of the master over the work of his assistants has to be presumed.

The Virtues and Vices (40 and 41 a-g)

For humanity, the Story of Salvation, which concludes with the *Last Judgment*, is a continual choice between virtue and vice. The contrast between the Virtues and the Vices, an iconographic theme with numerous precedents in medieval art, has an important literary source in Prudentius's *Psychomachia* or "Contest of the Soul" (early 5th century). It is highly likely that the text of the inscriptions located under the representations of Virtues and Vices, many of them now unfortunately worn away, had been supplied to the painter by a cultured scholar from the ecclesiastic circles of Padua. The sequence of the Virtues commences in the apsidal zone with the figure of *Prudence* and continues with *Fortitude, Temperance, Justice, Faith, Charity* and *Hope*.

With her mirror *Prudence* views the Past, portrayed at the back of her neck with the head of an old man. *Fortitude* grips a club and a shield, and her head and shoulders are covered with a lion skin. *Temperance* holds a sheathed sword and has a bit in her mouth as symbols of the need for restraint.

Justice is depicted with a pair of scales, in which she weighs good deeds on the right and bad deeds on the left. *Faith* holds the cross and the scroll of the holy scriptures, while trampling idols and false scriptures under her feet. *Charity* offers God her heart and in her right hand holds a basket of flowers and fruit, a symbol of love. At the same time she is trampling on bags of money. *Hope* is represented by a winged figure in flight who is about to receive a crown.

The sequence of Vices starts from the wall adjoining the apsidal zone with *Stupidity* and continues with *Inconstancy, Wrath, Injustice, Idolatry, Envy* and *Despair*. *Stupidity* is a jester, a symbol of madness. *Inconstancy* is a young woman balanced on a wheel and about to fall over backward. *Wrath* is rending her garments. *Injustice* is an old man with a sword and spear. At his feet are represented the effects of bad government: war, crime and pillage. *Idolatry*, tied to an idol, is unable to see or hear the sacred texts read by the prophet above.

Envy is blind, her tongue a serpent, and burns like fire. *Despair*, a suicide, is an extreme evil and the devil is already tearing her soul from her body. The allegorical figures, painted in monochrome, are set inside niches of mock marble. The most famous of them, *Charity, Justice* and *Hope*, were frequently imitated in 14th-century art. The representations of civil life in the allegories of *Justice* and *Injustice* are beautiful and the first examples in painting of the civilization that Ambrogio Lorenzetti was to depict on a large scale in the frescoes of the *Good Government* and *Bad Government* in the Palazzo Pubblico of Siena.

The Vault and the Decorative Bands (42 and 43)

The tunnel vault that roofs the chapel has been painted to simulate a starry sky, on which are set two tondi with a gold ground containing images of *Christ Pantocrator* and the *Madonna and Child*. There are also four smaller tondi surrounding the figure of Christ, in which are depicted the four prophets who foretold his birth: *Ezekiel, Jeremiah, Micah* and *Saint John the Baptist*. On the decorative band adjacent to the archway, ten *Patriarchs* are represented half-length, inside multifoil frames. The *Madonna and Child* are surrounded by tondi with a gold ground, in which are depicted the four prophets who predicted the divine motherhood of Mary: *Malachi, Baruch, Isaiah* and *Daniel*. In their left hands they hold scrolls bearing the text of their prophecies. On the decorative band adjacent to the façade and the one in the middle of the vault are represented *Kings, Patriarchs* and *Judges*, the progenitors of Mary according to the genealogy of the Old and New Testament. In the bands of decoration that separate the individual scenes on the first tier the *Apostles* are depicted half-length, inside

multifoil frames. At the ends of the second tier are set busts of *Saint Catherine of Alexandria, Saint Margaret of Antioch, Saint Lucy* and *Saint Elizabeth*. The four Evangelists (*Matthew, Mark, Luke* and *John*) and the four Doctors of the Church (*Gregory the Great, Jerome, Ambrose* and *Augustine*) are represented at the ends of the lower tier, in front of their desks. Episodes from the Old Testament related to the adjacent Gospel scene are depicted on the decorative bands separating the scenes on the north wall, establishing a close connection between the story from the New Testament and the one from the Old Testament that prefigures it. The scenes are *The Circumcision, Moses Strik-*

Madonna and Child,
detail of one of the
tondi on the vault,
prior to restoration

ing Water from the Rock, *The Creation of Adam*, *The Sons of the Prophets of Jericho Going to Meet the Prophet Elisha*, *The Archangel Michael Fighting the Dragon*, *Moses Raising the Serpent on the Cross*, *Moses Receiving the Tables of the Law*, *Jonah Swallowed by the Whale*, *Judah Son of Jacob*, *Elijah Carried Away by the Chariot of Fire* and *God Delivering a Scroll to the Prophet Ezekiel* (Bellinati 1975).

From the complex iconography it can be deduced that the choice of episodes is based on medieval biblical exegesis, St. Thomas Aquinas's *Summa Theologica* and the Christian Aristotelianism of the kind that is also to be found in Dante's *Divina Commedia*.

The Cycle of Frescoes: *Scenes from the Life of Mary*

In the area of the presbytery, long after Giotto's departure from Padua, an anonymous follower of the master painted scenes from the life of Mary based on the medieval text of the *Transitus Mariae*.

The narration runs from top to bottom, along the left-hand side wall and the right-hand one. In the first scene the angel foretells Mary's death: "Behold, said He a palm branch – I have brought it to thee from the paradise of the Lord – which thou wilt cause to be carried before thy bier, when on the third day thou shalt be taken up from the body." In the second scene the apostles make their last farewell to Mary: "all the apostles were snatched up, raised on a cloud." In the third Mary is dead and Jesus comes to fetch her soul: "He was lifted up on a cloud, and taken back into heaven, and the angels along with Him, carrying the blessed Mary into the paradise of God." In the fourth Mary's funeral is held and as the apostles are carrying her body, some men in Jerusalem took up arms to kill the apostles and burn the body of the Virgin. But they were suddenly struck by blindness and fell, beating one another against the walls. In the fifth the apostles place the body in the sepulcher, "and a great brightness came down upon that place [...] and kissing her, the Lord went back, and delivered her soul to the angels, that they should carry it into paradise."

In the sixth scene Mary is crowned by Christ in Heaven. The individual scenes are filled with figures, represented expressionistically in an attempt to convey emotions and sentiments. But this effort is not matched by the stylistic quality, with the result that the bodies look clumsy and the faces inexpressive. A late date is presumed for the frescoes, and in any case after 1317, since among the saints on the apsidal arch can be found St. Louis of Anjou, who was canonized on April 7, 1317. In fact they were probably executed after 1323, since another of the saints represented is Thomas of Aquinas, canonized on July 18, 1323.

The Sculptures of Giovanni Pisano

On the altar in the apse are set three marble sculptures signed "IOH.IS MAGISTRI NICOLI." Thus in these works Giovanni Pisano identified himself as the son of the sculptor Nicola.

The delicacy of the modeling, the Gothic elegance of the drapery and the intensity of the gaze exchanged by Mother and Child make the *Madonna* one of Giovanni's masterpieces. The two *Angels Holding Candles* are also signed by Giovanni, who presumably carved the three figures before 1305, the year in which the chapel was consecrated.

The high altar is original, although with a few modifications, and holds the relics of the consecration ceremony held on March 25, 1305.

Giovanni Pisano,
*Angels Holding
Candles*, statues
located alongside
the *Madonna*

The Tomb and Statue of Enrico Scrovegni

On March 22, 1336, Enrico Scrovegni, in exile in Venice, dictated a will in which he expressed a desire to be buried in the chapel he had built in Padua. He died on August 20 and on November 23 his remains were taken to Padua. The funerary urn must have been installed prior to 1320, the year in which Enrico was given asylum in Venice. However, the tombstone with the reclining figure of Scrovegni was executed after his death, perhaps using a death mask as a model.

The two sculptures have been attributed by some to Giovanni Pisano, by others to his workshop and by yet others to an anonymous Tuscan. Wolters ascribes them to the Venetian sculptor who carved the sepulchral monument to Castellano Salomone in Treviso Cathedral. Underneath Enrico's sarcophagus is located that of his wife Jacopina. The tombstones of several members of the Scrovegni family are set in the floor in front of the altar and behind it.

Furnishings and Frescoes of the Apse and Sacristy

In addition to the *Cross*, Scrovegni had provided the chapel with furnishings. Unfortunately nothing has survived of the 14th-century vestments, liturgical books and church ornaments. In the sacristy there is a large "cabinet" from the time as well as a fresco decoration on the walls dating from the middle of the 14th century. The wooden stalls in the nave date from the 16th century. Finally, among the "14th-century wooden stalls" in the apse, there are two works representing the same subject, the *Madonna and Child*: one can be ascribed to Giusto de' Menabuoi and the other to Jacopo da Verona. In the 19th century the *Crucifix* painted on wood now in the Museo Civico used to be set against the rear wall of the apse, above the sarcophagus of Enrico Scrovegni (Crowe, Cavalcaselle 1864). The large cross, painted on both sides, must originally have stood on a *pergula*.

The Restorations of the Chapel

No alterations have been made to the chapel since it was built and so Giotto's cycle of frescoes can be considered the best preserved work of his full maturity, subjected to no repaintings or restorations that might have damaged it as has happened with the frescoes he painted in the Bardi and Peruzzi Chapels in Florence. The only intervention took place in the 16th century, with the addition of a room with a loggia on top of the 14th-century sacristy to provide a link between the chapel and the palace of the Scrovegni family so that its members could attend services from the window opened in the apse.

The palace, whose architectural structure is recorded in Giovanni

Valle's *Plan of the City of Padua* (1784), was demolished in 1827. The portico built onto the front of the chapel in the 15th century collapsed in 1817 (Moschini 1817). The state of preservation of Giotto's frescoes was judged to be fairly good by Paduan historians (Rossetti 1765, Moschini 1826). In the city Pietro Selvatico argued for the need to tackle the problem of restoration, and was supported in this by Giovanni Battista Cavalcaselle, in Padua in the years 1857, 1864 and 1865 to study Giotto's frescoes and the Paduan painting of the 14th and 15th centuries, during which time he made a long series of drawings and annotations. The individual scenes of the cycle of frescoes were analyzed stylistically and the state of preservation of each recorded (Spiazzi 1983). The Commune of Padua set up a Commission and Selvatico and Cavalcaselle were *de facto* responsible for the methodology used in the investigations. Checks were made to establish the extent of deterioration of the masonry and the frescoes, with very precise graphical surveys, and decisions over the restorations to be carried out were taken (Prosdocimi 1960). The complete photographic documentation of the frescoes, suggested by Caval-

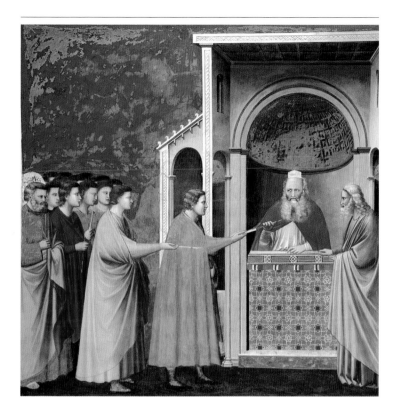

caselle and commissioned by the Commune from the Naya firm in Venice, constituted a methodologically exceptional example of planning for the time. In the meantime the Commune had opened negotiations for the purchase of the chapel from its owner, Foscari Grandenigo, and in 1880 it was acquired at a cost of 54,971 lire. The task of restoration, entrusted to Guglielmo Botti of Pisa in the years 1869-71, was then given to the Paduan restorer Antonio Bertolli, who had collaborated with Botti previously. The intervention took place over the period from 1881 to 1894. In an attempt to save the frescoes during the Second World War, three tondi depicting *Prophets* and the tondo with the *Madonna and Child* were detached from the ceiling, but the work was interrupted immediately afterward. In the years 1961-63 the roof was restored: the wooden trusses were replaced by metal ones, along with four collar beams on the inside that were badly decayed. The job of restoring the frescoes was entrusted to Leonetto Tintori (Tintori, Meiss 1961). In 1976 an earthquake left serious cracks in the walls, in the façade and in the vault where it adjoined the façade, and some parts of the band of decoration came away. Steps were immediately taken to repair the damage.

The damage caused by the earthquake of 1976 raised the problem of conservation again and the decision was taken to launch a program of studies and research coordinated by the Istituto Centrale di Restauro in collaboration with the Commune of Padua, the Soprintendenza ai Beni Artistici e Storici of the Veneto and the Soprintendenza ai Beni Architettonici e Ambientali of Eastern Veneto.

These studies provided confirmation that the cause of the decay was atmospheric pollution, through the process of sulfation, as had already been suggested by the chemical tests made during the restoration carried out in 1961-63 (Valcanover 1971).

The results of the investigations, published in a special issue of the *Bollettino d'Arte*, were summed up by Giovanni Urbani, director of the Istituto Centrale di Restauro, in a list of the measures to be taken: closure of the entrance to prevent the continuous introduction of polluted air; rehabilitation of the side door, close to the triumphal arch, and construction of a suitably air-conditioned ticket office; substitution of the lamps then in use with new lamps producing cold light; continual and constant routine maintenance.

The new entrance structure has now been completed, and a limit placed on the number of visitors allowed into the chapel at any one time. The control of the microclimate achieved by such interventions has made it possible to halt the deterioration of the frescoes, by removing its causes. The masonry of the façade has recently been restored. From 1988 to 1991 the Istituto carried out graphical surveys and urgent interventions in the painted surface. The sculptures of Giovanni Pisano have been restored and the painted plaster in the apsidal zone has been consolidated. Bringing the "microclimatic control unit" into operation and controlling its functioning for at least a year are the preconditions for starting on the complete restoration of the frescoes, from the elimination of sulfates to the consolidation of the coat of paint and its cleaning. The results of the scientific investigations conducted after 1983 by the members of the Commission set up by the Commune of Padua were made known in the course of a day of study (*La Cappella degli Scrovegni...*, 1998).

The Restorations of Giotto's Cycle

Giuseppe Basile

What is presented here is a visual record of Giotto's cycle following the restoration to which it has been subjected by the ICR. An intervention that commenced in July 2001 and was completed within the space of a few months, but for which detailed preparations had been made for around a quarter of a century. In fact the most recent history of the work can be said to date from the time when, at an international conference held in 1971, only eight years after Leonetto Tintori's restoration, the then head of the Soprintendenza, F. Valcanover, raised the alarm over the fact that some signs of damage to Giotto's frescoes were already visible.

The restoration had not been done badly, but the underestimation of the need to carry out regular checks and when necessary interventions of maintenance in the building and the environment, even before the paintings themselves, and above all the emergence of as serious a problem – for the purposes of conservation – as pollution was starting to become, meant that the deterioration of the frescoes had begun again. Indeed it had undergone an unexpected acceleration, if we consider that over sixty years had passed between Tintori's restoration and the previous one.

The damage inflicted on the chapel by the earthquake that devastated Friuli in 1976 had induced those responsible for the conservation of the monument to speed up the work, and in particular to ask the ICR to take charge of Giotto's cycle so that the restoration could be carried out systematically in order to ensure more lasting results. In effect the Istituto took an innovative approach to the problem of preserving Giotto's paintings, overturning the traditional practice of restoring the work of art independently of study of the environment and the building. Instead it decided to carry out a survey of any work

necessary to adapt and conserve these prior to intervening in the paintings themselves.

The method that was used to plan and execute the scientific investigations, broad in scope but also carefully targeted, is a procedure whose validity has now been amply demonstrated. The same is true of the articulated and progressive way in which the measures, from the most elementary to the most complicated, have been put into operation, moving from one step to the next only after the effectiveness of the results obtained had been verified.

Thus the interventions for improvement of the environment that were most easily implemented (installation of window screens, replacement of incandescent bulbs, etc.) were followed by measures to repair the building (carried out by the Commune of Padua) and finally the installation of a microclimatic control unit called the CTA (Corpo Tecnologico Attrezzato), a sort of filter between the interior of the monument and the external environment which represents the most complex and innovative type of intervention, developed for the first time expressly for the Scrovegni Chapel. The CTA was realized by the Commune of Padua to a design based on research conducted

by the interdisciplinary commission set up for the purpose, made up of representatives of the Commune, the Istituto Centrale di Restauro and the competent Soprintendenze and specialists from the university and the CNR.

A year then went by after the activation of the CTA, during which time the environmental situation inside the building was subject to monitoring by instruments to check the suitability of the measures taken. The results were positive and so it proved possible to take the steps required for the conservation and restoration of the paintings on the walls of the chapel, bringing to a halt the extremely grave process of deterioration consisting in the transformation of the painted plaster into gypsum, with a consequent pulverization of the paint.

The following criteria have been followed:

a) urgent interventions of conservation in the zones at greatest risk (the west wall with the *Last Judgment* and in particular the right-hand part depicting *Hell*; the third tier of the left-hand wall of the nave and the adjoining part of the vault; the two panels detached and reattached at the end of the 19th century, representing *Christ among the Doctors in the Temple* and *The Road to Calvary*; the third row of the left-hand wall of the presbytery, with the *Foretelling of Mary's*

Death, and the adjacent vault) and general conservation measures;
b) reduction of the differences in color resulting from previous interventions of restoration (Botti and Bertolli in the late 19th century, Tintori in the early 1960s).

With regard to point *a)* in particular, the following operations have been carried out:

1 consolidation of the preparatory layers;

2 extraction of salts (and concurrent reconstitution of the adhesion of the coat of paint in the zones treated with synthetic resins that had not been fully tested in the restoration of 1957-63);

3 removal of coherent and incoherent material deposited on the surface of the paint over the course of time (atmospheric dust), or applied for the purposes of conservation (to "fix" the coat of paint) or aesthetic reasons (coloring of the "neutral" areas of plaster) but which has now undergone alteration;

4 treatment to conserve the 3200 nails used at the end of the 19th century to anchor the areas of plaster that had come away from the wall by isolation of the head and replacement of the plaster above.

With regard to point *b)*, the most important aspects, owing to the size of the areas involved, concern the missing blue background and the gaps in the plaster that had been filled during earlier restorations. The gaps in the blue background have been "dimmed," i.e. optically toned down so that they are less noticeable to the observer, but without replacing the missing paint, and an attempt has been made to give the replastered areas as homogeneous an appearance as possible, so that they do not interfere with the overall effect.

In particularly significant cases (such as the painted architecture which provides a framework for the whole of the decoration, holding the "panels") the gaps have been filled by "hatching" in watercolor, as is the usual practice when dealing with such lacunae.

The most important example of the reintegration of gaps by "hatching" is the triumphal arch, and in particular the upper part, where *God the Father Instructing the Archangel Gabriel to Make the Announcement to Mary* and the *Annunciation* are represented.

This is the most badly damaged part of the whole chapel (along with the *Last Judgment* on the west wall) as a result of the collapse (1824) of the adjoining palace, which had supported it. Extensive repair work carried out at the end of the 19th century was able to keep the building from falling down, but of course could not eliminate the damage.

This damage affected the pictorial decoration as well, and in photographs taken at the time the bare wall is visible at many points.

These areas, where all the layers of the decoration (coat of paint, plaster) were missing, have been treated in two ways:

1 by restoring the mock architectural elements (on the triumphal arch) where they no longer exist, repainting them in tempera;

2 in all other cases, by filling the lacunae with mortar and painting them a "neutral" color with tempera, which not only makes no attempt to recreate the lost image but distinguishes them as clearly as possible from the original painting.

In the current intervention we have decided to stick with the 19th-century decision to restore the pictorial continuity of the mock architecture (an interrupted work of architecture is not "credible"), but – obviously – using a more suitable method that makes it possible to meet conflicting requirements: restoring the integrity of the original image but employing a technique ("hatching") that makes the intervention instantly recognizable (no one has ever painted or would ever paint on a wall – and in watercolor at that – in thin, straight vertical strokes that in no way follow the original lines of the decoration).

The "optical dimming" of the gaps has been resorted to much more widely, in practice in all those areas where the mock architectural framework of the chapel (baseboard of imitation marble with the *Vices* and *Virtues*, pilasters and pilaster strips that run from the bottom to the vault of the building at the top) is not present, with the exception of a few extremely limited and well-defined parts in which the use of "hatching" proved necessary either for figurative reasons (to avoid as far as possible interference with the legibility of the image) or out of methodological consistency (in order not to interrupt a lacuna in an artificial manner by treating parts of it differently, depending on whether they affected the mock architecture of the chapel or not).

This method of reintegration of the gaps has also been applied in the most heavily deteriorated zones, the ones in which the most that could be hoped for was to reduce the visual disturbance caused by the very poor state of preservation and the previous work of restoration: the *Elect* and the *Blessed* on the west wall, the *Wedding Procession* and, above all, the panels depicting *Christ among the Doctors* and *The Road to Calvary*, which had deteriorated to such an extent by the end of the 19th century that it had been necessary to remove them from the natural support of the wall and apply them to new, removable backings set in braided brass wire and mortar.

Naturally, the aim of this second aspect of the restoration has been to re-create as far as possible the original pictorial text, and in particular (given that it had been neglected in the past) the unity of the two "supporting" elements of the entire decoration: the mock archi-

tecture and the blue background present everywhere except on the baseboard and in the depiction of *Hell*.

It is my hope that the intervention will facilitate perception of the complexity and novelty of Giotto's work, from both the technical point of view (the rediscovery of *marmorino* or Roman stucco used to imitate marble, the employment of oil for certain pigments) and the formal one (in particular the restoration of the chromatic and not just the plastic and volumetric value of the images as well as the accentuation of the dynamic and "theatrical" structure of the pictorial space of the chapel, in part through the discovery of previously overlooked details such as the pieces of mirror inserted in Christ's halo in the *Last Judgment*).

The restoration has been extended to include all the other artworks in the chapel (except the wooden stalls) and thus, in addition to the wooden panel with the *Eternal*, to Giovanni Pisano's *Madonna and Child* and two *Angels Holding Candles*, to the statue of Enrico praying and his sepulchral monument, to the mural paintings in the apse and the presbytery, to the three-light window and to the other furnishings and fittings.

Principal Structural Characteristics of the Scrovegni Chapel

Serenella Borsella

As is well-known, the Scrovegni Chapel, a small and simple brick building with a pitched roof, stands inside the area of Padua's Roman amphitheater, commonly referred to as the Arena, of which considerable parts are still standing and with which it shares, according to the reconstruction made by Brunelli Bonetti in 1907, a number of architectural and structural elements of the façade, which follows the line of the elliptical outer wall, and the longitudinal boundary walls, which appear to be founded on partitions radiating from the wall itself.

According to Brunelli Bonetti's reconstructions the Arena, whose main axis ran in a northeast/southwest direction, measured 134.26 × 97.31 m on the outside and 76.40 × 39.45 m on the inside, forming a slightly squashed ellipse.

The chapel consists of a single nave measuring 21.5 × 8.5 m in plan and 8.5 m high, a small presbytery and an apsidal zone, of polygonal shape and without a transept, facing east and separated from the nave by a stone archway. A small sacristy is set against the northeast corner, adjacent to the presbytery. However, neither the apse nor the sacristy appear to have been part of the original structure of the chapel.

The chapel's outer walls, built out of solid bricks, are 67 cm thick (78 cm in correspondence with the pilasters). They extend 8.5 m above the floor and 90 cm below it, while the floor of the nave is set on top of a 27-cm-thick segmental vault of solid brick (Eng. Modena) which also forms the ceiling of the crypt underneath.

The nave is covered by a tunnel vault of double-headed solid bricks, held by five steel collar beams installed in 1963 to replace the original ones and anchored externally to the longitudinal outer walls by steel plates again.

Roman amphitheater
of Padua, plan
of the archeological
excavations carried
out between 1880
and 1907

Facing page,
plan and sections
of the chapel

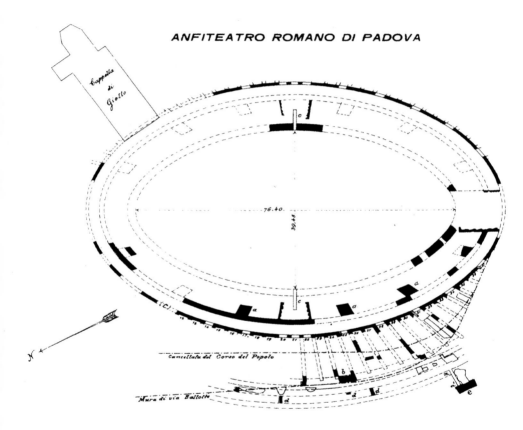

ANFITEATRO ROMANO DI PADOVA

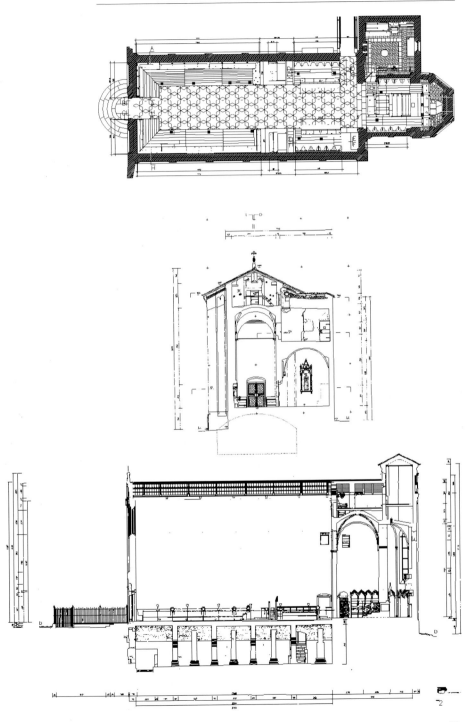

81

The original wooden roof of the nave, with wooden trusses resting directly on the brick vault frescoed by Giotto, was replaced in 1967 and the original wooden trusses were replaced by eight steel trusses, although these now rest solely on the longitudinal outer walls by means of a new stringcourse of reinforced concrete.

The presbytery, separated from the apse and the nave by two stone arches, is roofed, like the apsidal conch, by a cross vault of solid brick. The octagonal turret on top is roofed by a brick cupola.

Both the former loggia, which was once connected to the palace demolished in the 19th century and which has now been blocked up and is no longer accessible, and the sacristy underneath have an almost square plan. They have vaulted and frescoed ceilings of solid brick. The floor under the terminal part of the roof was also replaced in the 1960s by a brick and concrete slab. The pitched roofs of the loggia and presbytery were rebuilt with concrete rafters and steel ties. Located right underneath the nave of the chapel and of the same dimensions, there is a basement, known as the cenoby, but this can only be entered from the outside by means of a narrow stone staircase.

The cenoby, which is still partially filled with massive partition walls constructed at the beginning of the last world war to protect the chapel from possible damage, has a brick vault whose underside is frescoed with a pale starry sky, mirroring the one painted by Giotto on the vault of the nave above. The remains of plastering decorated with large, monochrome, geometric panels can still be seen on the walls. The floor, in Venetian *seminato* with orange tones probably dating from the end of the 19th century, when a layer of over one meter of earth was removed, slopes slightly to the southwest. It is set about 3 m below the level of the surrounding ground and about 4.55 m below the floor of the nave above.

Bibliography

Bandera Bistoletti, S., *Giotto*, Firenze 1989.

Banzaro, D. (ed.), *La Croce di Giotto. Il restauro*, Milano 1995.

Basile, G. and Magro, P.P. (eds.), *Il cantiere pittorico della basilica superiore di San Francesco di Assisi*, Assisi 2001.

Bellinati, C., "La Cappella di Giotto e le miniature dell'Antifonario 'giottesco' della cattedrale (1306)," in *Da Giotto al Mantegna*, exhibition catalogue, Padova 1974, pp. 28-80.

Bellinati, C., "La cappella degli Scrovegni," in *Padua, Basiliche e Chiese*, Vicenza 1975.

Bellinati, C., *Giotto. Atlante iconografico della Cappella di Giotto (1300-1305)*, Treviso 1997.

Bellosi, L., *Giotto*, Firenze 1982.

Bellosi, L., *La pecora di Giotto*, Torino 1985.

Bologna, F., *Novità su Giotto. Giotto al tempo della cappella Peruzzi*, Torino 1969.

Bonsanti, G., *Giotto*, Padova 1985.

Ciatti, M. and Seidel, M. (eds.), *Giotto, la Croce di Santa Maria Novella*, Firenze 2001.

Colabich, G.F., Prosdocimi, A. and Saccomani, G., *I recenti lavori di restauro alla Cappella degli Scrovegni e le indagini esperite per la sua conservazione*, Padova 1964.

Crowe, J.A. and Cavalcaselle, G.B., *A New History of Painting in Italy*, vol. I, London 1864.

Flores d'Arcais, F., "Affreschi giotteschi nella Basilica del Santo a Padua," in *Critica d'Arte*, no. 97, 1968, pp. 23-33.

Flores d'Arcais, F., "Il miniatore degli Antifonari della Cattedrale di Padova: datazioni e attribuzioni," in *Bollettino del Museo Civico di Padova*, 1974, pp. 25-59.

Flores d'Arcais, F., *Giotto*, Milan 1995.

Ghiberti, L., *I commentari* (*c.* 1450), ed. by J. von Schlosser, Berlin 1912.

Gioseffi, D., *Giotto architetto*, Milano 1968.

"Giotto a Padova," in *Bollettino d'Arte*, special series, no. 2, 1983.

Giotto e il suo tempo. Atti del Congresso internazionale per il VII centenario della nascita di Giotto (1967), Roma 1971.

Giovanni da Nono, *Visio Aegidii Regio Patavi* (*c.* 1340-50), ed. by G. Fabris, "La Cronaca di Giovanni da Nono," in *Bollettino del Museo Civico di Padova*, special issue, VIII, 1938.

Gnudi, C., "Il passo di Riccobaldo Ferrarese relativo a Giotto e il problema della sua autenticità," in *Studies in the History of Art: dedicated to William E. Suida*, London 1959, pp. 26-30.

Gnudi, C., *Giotto*, Milano 1959.

Gnudi, C., "Sugli inizi di Giotto e i suoi rapporti col mondo gotico," in *Giotto e il suo tempo...*, cit.

Imdal, M., *Giotto Arenafresken. Ikonographie - Ikonologie - Ikonik*, München 1980.

La Cappella degli Scrovegni. Indagini, restauri, interventi, proceedings of the day of study, February 25, 1998, Padova 1998.

Longhi, R., "Giotto spazioso," in *Paragone*, 31 (1952), pp. 18-24.

Meiss, M., *Giotto and Assisi*, New York 1960 (repr. 1967).

Moschetti, A., "La distrutta iconostasi alla cappella Scrovegni," in *Atti e Memorie dell'Accademia di SS.LL.AA. di Padua*, XXXIX (1922-23), pp. 177-83.

Moschini, G., *Guida per la Città di Padova*, Venezia 1817.

Moschini, G., *Delle origini e delle vicende della Pittura in Padova*, Padova 1826.

Oertel, R., "Wende der Giotto-Vorschung," in *Zeitschrift für Kunstgeschichte*, XI (1943-44), pp. 1-27.

Offner, R., "Giotto, non Giotto," in *The Burlington Magazine*, LXXIV (1939), pp. 259-68; LXXV (1940), pp. 96-113.

Palumbo, G., *Giotto e i giotteschi in Assisi*, Roma 1969.

Previtali, G., *Giotto e la sua bottega*, Milano 1967 (2nd ed. 1974).

Prosdocimi, A., "Il Comune di Padova e la Cappella degli Scrovegni nell'Ottocento," in *Bollettino del Museo Civico di Padova*, XLIX, no. 1 (1960).

Riccobaldo Ferrarese, *Compilatio Chronologica* (*c.* 1312-13), in L.A. Muratori, *Rerum Italicarum Scriptores*, tome IX, Milano 1726.

Rintelen, F., *Giotto und die Giotto-Apokryphen*, München-Leipzig 1912.

Romanini, A.M., "Gli occhi di Isacco. Classicismo e curiosità scientifica tra Arnolfo e Giotto," in *Arte Medievale*, I-II, pp. 1-43.

Ronchi, O., "Un documento inedito del 9 gennaio 1305 intorno alla Cappella degli Scrovegni," in *Atti e Memorie dell'Accademia di SS.LL.AA. di Padua*, LII, tome II, Padova, 1935-36, pp. 205-11.

Rossetti, G.B., *Descrizione delle Pitture, Sculture, ed Architetture di Padova*, Padova 1765.

Salvini, R., *Giotto. Bibliografia*, Roma 1938.

Salvini, R., *Tutta la Pittura di Giotto*, Milano 1962.

Salvini, R. and De Benedetti, C., *Giotto. Bibliografia*, Roma 1970.

Savonarola, M., *Commentariolus de laudibus Patavis* (*c.* 1440), in L.A. Muratori, *Rerum Italicarum Scriptores*, tome XXIV, Milano 1738.

Schlegel, U., "Zum Bildprogramm der Arena-Kapelle," in *Zeitschrift für Kunstgeschichte*, 1957.

Sgarbi, V. (ed.), *Giotto e il suo tempo*, exhibition catalogue, Milano 2000.

Spiazzi, A.M., "Giotto a Padova. I restauri della Cappella degli Scrovegni nei secoli XIX e XX," in "Giotto a Padova," cit.

Spiazzi, A.M., "Padova," in *La Pittura nel Veneto. Il Trecento*, vol. I, Milano 1992, pp. 88-177.

Tartuferi, A. (ed.), *Giotto. Bilancio critico di sessant'anni di studio e ricerche*, exhibition catalogue, Firenze 2000.

Thode, H., *Giotto*, Bielefeld-Leipzig, 1899.

Thomas, H.M., "La missione di Gabriele nell'affresco di Giotto alla Cappella degli Scrovegni a Padova," in *Bollettino del Museo Civico di Padova*, LXXXVI, 1987 (1989), pp. 99-112.

Tintori, L., "Il bianco di piombo nelle pitture murali di San Francesco ad Assisi," in *Studies in Mediaeval and Renaissance Painting in Honor of M. Meiss*, New York 1977.

Tintori, L. and Meiss, M., *The Painting of the Life of St. Francis in Assisi*, New York 1961.

Toesca, P., "Gli antichi affreschi di Santa Maria Maggiore," in *L'Arte*, VII, 1904, pp. 312-17.

Toesca, P., *Giotto*, Torino 1941.

Tolomei, A., "La Cappella degli Scrovegni all'Arena di Padova," in *idem*, *Scritti vari*, Padova 1880.

Tolomei, A., *La Chiesa di Santa Maria della Carità dipinta da Giotto*, Padova 1884.

Tomei, A., *Jacopus Torriti pictor. Una vicenda figurativa del tardo Duecento romano*, Roma 1990.

Urbani, G., "Studi sullo stato di conservazione della Cappella degli Scrovegni di Padova," in *Bollettino d'Arte*, special series, no. 63 (1978), p. 147.

Valcanover, F., "Le cause del rapido deterioramento degli affreschi della Cappella Scrovegni negli ultimi venti anni," in *Giotto e il suo tempo*, cit.

Vasari, G., *Le Vite...*, ed. by R. Bettarini and P. Barocchi, text and commentary with comparison between the two editions, Firenze 1966-67. Eng. ed. *Lives of the Artists*, trans. by G. Bull, Harmondsworth 1965.

Volpe, C., "Il lungo percorso del 'dipingere dolcissimo e tanto unito'," in *Storia dell'Arte Italiana*, vol. I, tome II, Torino 1983, pp. 232-308.

Zanardi, B., Zeri, F. and Frugoni, C., *Il cantiere di Giotto. La storia di San Francesco ad Assisi*, Milano 1996.

On following page,
Master of the Scrovegni and Salomone Tombs,
Statue of Enrico Scrovegni (1336-39)